Raindrops
Fall All Around

by
Charles Ghigna

illustrated by
Laura Watson

PICTURE WINDOW BOOKS
a capstone imprint

In the country, in the town ...

rain is falling all around.

Raindrops drip on leaves and flowers.

Cars splash through the April showers.

Raindrops keep a steady beat.

Rain forms puddles in the street.

Rain turns hillsides fresh and green.

Raindrops wash the sidewalks clean.

A flowing creek fills up with rain.

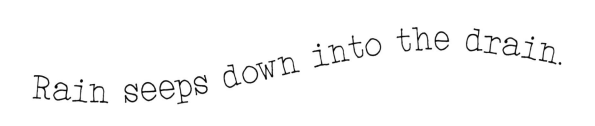

Rain seeps down into the drain.

Rushing water makes a path.

Bluebirds take a little bath.

Ducklings swim around the lake.

Raindrops make the puppies shake.

Lightning flashes in the sky.

Thunder rumbles way up high.

Time to say goodnight to rain.

Raindrops tap-dance on the pane.

Rain clouds slowly pass on by.

A rainbow spreads across the sky.

All About Rain

- Rain is a kind of precipitation. Precipitation is rain, snow, sleet, or hail that falls from clouds to the ground.
- Did you know that the water in a puddle could have once been in your drinking glass? The water cycle makes this possible. Rain falls from clouds to the earth as part of the water cycle. Take a look at the water cycle:

condensation — gas turns into water

evaporation — water turns into gas

precipitation — water, snow, or ice falls

water collection on the ground

- Tiny raindrops are called drizzle.
- People can measure rainfall with a tool called a rain gauge.
- When a lot of rain falls all at once, flooding can happen. Flooding happens when water covers up what is normally dry land.
- Scientists use tools to help predict weather. To predict means to tell what something may be like in the future.

weather radar station — uses radar to predict weather

anemometer (a-nuh-MOM-uh-tuhr) — measures wind speed and direction

All the Titles in This Set:

Hail to Spring!

Raindrops Fall All Around

Sunshine Brightens Springtime

A Windy Day in Spring

Internet Sites

FactHound offers a safe, fun way to find Internet sites related to this book. All of the sites on FactHound have been researched by our staff.

Here's all you do:

Visit *www.facthound.com*

Type in this code: 9781479560301

Super-cool stuff! Check out projects, games and lots more at
www.capstonekids.com

For Charlotte and Christopher.

Thanks to our adviser for his expertise, research, and advice:
Terry Flaherty, PhD, Professor of English
Minnesota State University, Mankato

Editors: Shelly Lyons and Elizabeth R. Johnson
Designer: Lori Bye
Art Director: Nathan Gassman
Production Specialist: Tori Abraham

The illustrations in this book were created with acrylics and digital collage.

Picture Window Books are published by Capstone,
1710 Roe Crest Drive, North Mankato, Minnesota 56003
www.capstonepub.com

Library of Congress Cataloging-in-Publication Data
Ghigna, Charles, author.
Raindrops fall all around / by Charles Ghigna ;
illustrated by Laura Watson.
pages cm. — (Nonfiction picture books. Springtime weather wonders)
   Summary: "Introduces rain through fun, poetic text and colorful illustrations"—Provided by publisher.
   Audience: Ages 5-7.
   Audience: K to grade 3.
ISBN 978-1-4795-6030-1 (library binding : alk. paper)
ISBN 978-1-4795-6034-9 (big book)
ISBN 978-1-4795-6038-7 (ebook pdf)
ISBN 978-1-4795-6042-4 (board book)
1. Spring—Juvenile literature. 2. Rain and rainfall—Juvenile literature. 3. Weather—Juvenile literature.
I. Watson, Laura, 1968- illustrator. II. Title.

Design Elements
Shutterstock: Mishkin_med

QB637.5.G484 2015
508.2—dc23   2014028999

Printed in Canada.
092014   008478FRS15